BATTLING EXTINCTION

Follow the Clues

by Tamra B. Orr

CHERRY LAKE PUBLISHING · ANN ARBOR, MICHIGAN

CHERRY LAKE Publishing

Published in the United States of America by Cherry Lake Publishing
Ann Arbor, Michigan
www.cherrylakepublishing.com

CONTENT EDITOR: Robert Wolffe, EdD, Professor of Teacher Education, Bradley University, Peoria, Illinois
BOOK DESIGN AND ILLUSTRATION: The Design Lab
READING ADVISER: Marla Conn, ReadAbility, Inc.

PHOTO CREDITS: Cover and pages 1, 5, and 10; ©Critterbiz/Shutterstock, Inc.; page 4, Paul K Cascio , U.S. Geological Survey; page 6, ©Mark Schwettmann/Shutterstock, Inc.; page 7, ©Donald Bowers Photography/ Shutterstock, Inc.; page 8, ©qingqing/Shutterstock, Inc.; page 11, ©iStockphoto.com/Westphalia; pages 12 and 26, ©Bas Meelker/Alamy; page 13, ©bikeriderlondon/Shutterstock, Inc.; pages 15 and 28, ©Danita Delimont/Alamy; page 16, ©SCOTT E NELSON/Shutterstock, Inc.; page 17, ©Blend Images/Shutterstock, Inc.; page 18, ©R. Gino Santa Maria/Shutterstock, Inc.; page 19, ©Kondor83/Shutterstock, Inc.; page 20, ©salajean/Shutterstock, Inc.; page 21, ©Diana Valujeva/Shutterstock, Inc.; page 22, ©O.Bellini/Shutterstock, Inc.; page 23, ©Al Mueller/Shutterstock, Inc.; page 24, ©luchschen/Shutterstock, Inc.; pages 25 and 27, ©ZUMA Press, Inc./Alamy; page 29, ©iStockphoto.com/AlexanderZam.

LIBRARY OF CONGRESS CATALOGING-IN-PUBLICATION DATA
Orr, Tamra, author.
Battling extinction / by Tamra B. Orr.
pages cm. — (Science explorer) (Follow the clues)
Summary: "Find out how the scientific method can be used to help the endangered whooping crane from going extinct." — Provided by publisher.
Audience: Grades 4 to 6.
Includes bibliographical references and index.
ISBN 978-1-62431-780-4 (lib. bdg.) — ISBN 978-1-62431-790-3 (pbk.) —
ISBN 978-1-62431-810-8 (ebook) — ISBN 978-1-62431-800-9 (pdf)
1. Whooping crane—Juvenile literature. 2. Extinction (Biology)—Juvenile literature. 3. Endangered species—Juvenile literature. 4. Wildlife conservation—Juvenile literature. I. Title.

QL696.G84O77 2014
639.97'832—dc23   2013045290

Cherry Lake Publishing would like to acknowledge the work of The Partnership for 21st Century Skills.
Please visit www.p21.org for more information.

Printed in the United States of America, Corporate Graphics Inc.
January 2014

TABLE OF CONTENTS

CHAPTER 1

AN EXCITING BEGINNING

A wildlife biologist helps feed baby whooping cranes.

"Wait until I tell you what the birds did today!" said Mr. Constantine, walking through the front door. Nathan grinned. He knew a lot of fathers came home at night with stories about work, but he doubted any of those stories were as exciting as his dad's. His father was a wildlife biologist. He spent a great deal of time at Maryland's Patuxent Wildlife Research Center studying **endangered** species. He always had a funny story or a surprising fact to share with Nathan when he came home at night.

Mr. Constantine's favorite species was the whooping crane. His passion for it made it Nathan's favorite, too. Nathan loved hearing stories about what the cranes at the center had done that day. When these birds picked a partner, they would do the most amazing dance. Whooping cranes stay with their partners for the rest of their lives. Mr. Constantine started to tell Nathan about the dance, but Nathan interrupted.

"There's one thing I don't understand, Dad," Nathan said. "Years ago, there were only a handful of these cranes left in the world. Although things are much better today, what happened to make the whoopers endangered in the first place?"

Whooping cranes mate for life.

"Excellent question, Nate!" replied Mr. Constantine. "The answer to that is HIPPO." He laughed at the confused look on his son's face.

"HIPPO is a word that helps you remember the different ways a species can become endangered. The *H* stands for '**habitat** loss.' Much of the wetlands where cranes like to live have been drained to make room for people's homes, crops, and livestock," explained Mr. Constantine.

"*I* is for 'introduced species.' That refers to a plant or animal that is not native to an area, but is brought into it and thrives," continued Mr. Constantine. "This can disturb the area's natural balance. The new species might eat another species' food or prey on the native animals that cannot protect themselves. This has not been a major obstacle for whooping cranes, but it has for many other species."

Wetlands are an important habitat for many different species.

Earth's human population is always growing.

"I bet the first *P* stands for 'pollution,' such as **pesticides** and accidental oil spills," said Nathan.

"That's right," agreed Mr. Constantine. "These substances can poison water and food supplies. They can also make an area impossible for creatures to live in. The second *P* stands for 'population'—too much of it! As the world's human population grows, it demands more land and more resources, which leaves less and less for animals.

"Finally, there is *O* for 'overhunting,'" Mr. Constantine continued. "This presented the biggest challenge for whooping cranes. They were hunted for their meat, and their white feathers were used for decorating women's hats and clothing. Sometimes the birds' eggs were stolen and sold illegally.

Whooping cranes were once hunted for their long, beautiful feathers.

By the early 1940s, experts estimated there were only 15 left in the entire world. People were worried the birds would become **extinct**."

The two of them were silent for a moment, feeling sad about the cranes. Then Mr. Constantine said, "Experts studied the birds and figured out what needed to be done to protect the species. Refuges were built to protect the birds. Places like the Patuxent Center focus on helping keep baby chicks safe until they are ready to be introduced to the wild. Thanks to those efforts, the world has hundreds of cranes now."

Mr. Constantine paused, then smiled. "We are hoping that after Big Lou and Peony's dance today, we will see eggs soon. The eggs would hatch in about a month," he added.

"Great! I can't wait to see the baby chicks," said Nathan.

GETTING A TICKET TO THE CRANE DANCE

Cranes can grow as tall as 5 feet (1.5 meters). They are the tallest birds in all of North America. When spread out, their wings can stretch 5 to 8 feet (1.5 to 2.4 m) across! Cranes are almost completely white, with a red **crown** and black on the tips of their feathers. They have long, sharp beaks and gold eyes. Cranes make very loud honking noises, earning them the nickname whoopers.

The key to mating in the world of whooping cranes is dancing really well. A male crane marches around with its feathers puffed out. It growls, pounds the ground with its feet, and tosses its head. All of these movements are the bird's way of saying, "Let's dance." If the female crane is interested, she starts dancing back, imitating the same motions. The birds stretch out their necks, fluff out their wings, and jump up high into the air. Next, the two add a little singing to the performance, calling out to each other with loud honks and whistles designed to help the couple bond. Once the two decide to be partners, they often bow, run in circles, and even throw sticks in the air. Cranes tend to mate for life, so when choosing a partner, they take those dance moves seriously.

CHAPTER 2

WELCOMING THE WHOOPERS!

↖ Whooping crane mates take turns caring for their eggs.

Before Nathan knew it, a month had flown by. One day, his father came home from the center incredibly excited. After days of being watched very carefully, Big Lou and Peony's two eggs were hatching.

"Hatching began yesterday," Mr. Constantine explained. "At first, there was this little pecking noise coming from the **clutch** of eggs. It was the sound of the chicks' beaks hitting the inside of the shells. Then, this

morning, both of them broke through. By tomorrow morning, they will be all the way out and napping. Hatching is exhausting work!"

Everyone at the center knew it was important that the cranes never get used to being around humans. It would make life too dangerous when the cranes were released in the wild. To disguise themselves, workers at the center wore a big, baggy white costume and a hood. One arm of the costume looked like the head of a crane and was used to hand out food or teach the chicks how to search for food. When Nathan visited the wildlife center, he watched from the **blind**, a wooden shed that hid him from the birds.

This person wears a baggy costume and crane head puppet to feed a young whooping crane.

By the time the two chicks had hatched, Nathan had names all ready. "The girl is Mabel," he said. "The boy is Sheldon." Mr. Constantine smiled. He liked the names.

A few days later, however, Mr. Constantine came home from the center and was definitely not smiling. "One of the chicks is not doing very well," he said. "She is moving very slowly and doesn't look good. We are a little worried about her." He sighed.

"I know what we can do," Nathan said. "Why don't we use the scientific method to figure out what's wrong?"

Whooping crane chicks are born covered in fluffy, golden down feathers.

The scientific method is used by all kinds of scientists.

THE SCIENTIFIC METHOD
1. Ask a question
2. Gather information and observe/research
3. Make a **hypothesis**—or guess the answer
4. Experiment to test your hypothesis
5. Analyze your test results
6. Present a conclusion

Nathan had learned about the scientific method in school, but he had been hearing about it from his father for years before that. It has six steps to it. With those six steps, scientists had been solving puzzles that had mystified people for years.

Mr. Constantine nodded in agreement. Nathan went to the hallway and got his jacket. "Let's go to the center and find a way to help Mabel."

How far will some wildlife biologists go to help the animals they work with? In the case of Dr. George Archibald, the answer is very far! In 1975, a female whooper named Tex came to the International Crane Foundation. She had been hand raised by humans at the San Antonio Zoo. She knew nothing about other whoopers or how to behave like one. When a male whooper was brought to her, Tex preferred the human handlers to him.

Dr. Archibald had an idea. Maybe he could perform the courtship dance with Tex. This would help her body prepare to lay eggs. Scientists would then **artificially fertilize** the eggs so that chicks would develop inside.

Dr. Archibald moved in with the bird for months, creating a relationship so that Tex would bond with him. He danced with her often, imitating the movements cranes make with their wings, plus jumping, twirling, and honking. Tex thought that she was the biologist's girlfriend! It took years before one of her eggs successfully hatched a healthy chick. The chick, a male, was named Gee Whiz. He has gone on to father many more generations of cranes.

Dr. Archibald founded the International Crane Foundation in Wisconsin in 1973. He has been given many international awards for his work—which included daily dances—to save the whoopers!

↰ Whooping crane chicks, just like any other animal, need water to stay healthy.

"I've been watching Mabel for the last few days," Mr. Constantine began. "At first she just seemed unusually tired. Then she almost completely stopped eating." He showed Nathan some pictures of Mabel. "Her eyes don't look bright like they did when she was born," he pointed out.

"When we put those clues together, it points to one problem," said the biologist. "I believe that Mabel is **dehydrated**." Nathan looked confused. "That means she is not drinking enough water, and it is making her sick," his father explained.

Whooping crane chicks learn a lot by watching and copying their parents or other adult cranes.

"But you always have plenty of fresh water for the birds," Nathan objected. "You replace it at least once a day. And cranes are waterbirds, so don't they naturally take a drink whenever they need one?"

Mr. Constantine nodded his head. "You would think so, Nate. But we have watched videos of many wild birds, including whooping cranes. And we have learned that it can take hours of coaxing and modeling to teach chicks to take sips of water."

Mr. Constantine thought about what they could do to teach the chick this skill. "Do you remember the first step of the scientific method?" he asked.

"Of course! We start with a question," Nathan replied. "This one is easy. How do we get Mabel to drink? What's next, Dad?"

"Step two is always observing and gathering information," replied Mr. Constantine. "I have some materials in my office. We should find most of the information we need there."

Nathan and his father spent the next hour reading through the center's materials on whooper chicks. "I want to find a natural way to help Mabel drink. I would rather not have to bring her in and use tubes and needles," said Mr. Constantine.

Together, they made a list of ways to help teach the chick to drink water. "Tomorrow morning I will have the staff start trying each method," said Nathan's father. "We will see what works best and if Mabel starts to feel better."

It is a good idea to take notes as you do research, whether in a notebook or on a computer.

"So," said Nathan, "the next step is forming a hypothesis, right?" His father nodded. "We know all of these ways to make a chick drink water. How does that information help us form a hypothesis?"

"We don't know for certain which of these methods will work for Mabel," said Mr. Constantine. "Each whooper is unique, just like people. What works for some whooper chicks will not work for others. What's the first method on our list?"

Each whooping crane needs different kinds of care and attention.

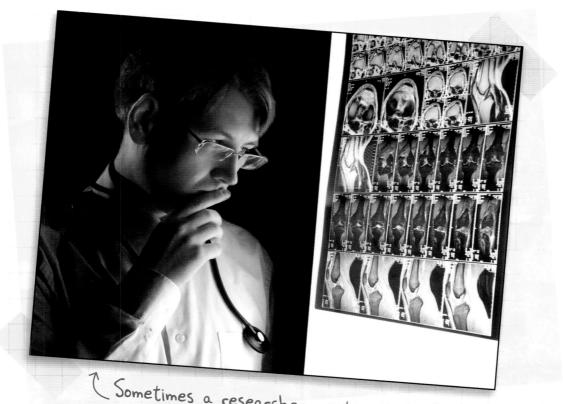

Sometimes a researcher must go back to the beginning and rethink a hypothesis.

Nathan looked at the list. "Use a puppet and encourage the chick to drink," he said.

"That will be our first hypothesis. Which means—"

"Experiment!" the two of them said together. Nathan grinned. This step was definitely his favorite part of the scientific method.

"We will test our hypothesis and analyze the results," continued Mr. Constantine. "If that hypothesis is proven false, we'll have to go back and change it."

"Scientific method, here we come!" Nathan exclaimed.

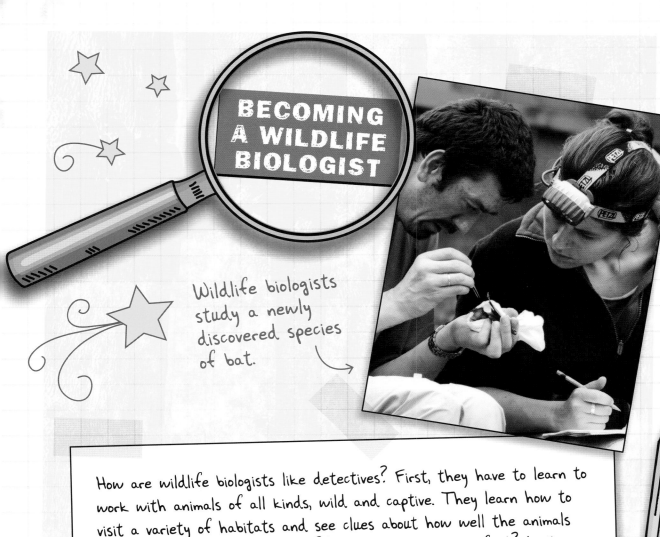

BECOMING A WILDLIFE BIOLOGIST

Wildlife biologists study a newly discovered species of bat.

How are wildlife biologists like detectives? First, they have to learn to work with animals of all kinds, wild and captive. They learn how to visit a variety of habitats and see clues about how well the animals are doing. Are they reproducing? Do they have enough food? Is their shelter safe? This might mean traveling to the desert for one project, then heading out to the mountains or the ocean for the next.

Like detectives, biologists do a great deal of research. They take measurements, make calculations, and keep detailed records. All of this study may help endangered species, like the whooping crane. Jobs for wildlife biologists are expected to grow steadily over the next few years. Start brushing up on those science classes now if you are interested in becoming one!

CHAPTER 4

MIXING MABEL AND THE SCIENTIFIC METHOD

"There are several different ways to help teach the baby chick to take a drink," Mr. Constantine explained to Nathan and the rest of the center staff the following morning. "I know some of you already know this information, but a few of you are new, so I wanted to review the details."

He pointed to a whiteboard with a list of steps on it and continued. "The first way is to put on the costume, and then use the head of the

Often, staff members take notes to help remember details from meetings.

↳ A glass marble is one way to catch a crane chick's attention.

crane puppet to lure the chick over to the bucket of water. Dip the tip of the puppet beak into the water. Allow the water to drip off it to get the chick's attention. This may be enough to get the little one to give it a try.

"Another technique is a little simpler," continued Mr. Constantine. "We can place something shiny in the water bowl to grab the bird's attention. Like other birds, whoopers are attracted to things that are shiny. Some centers use live insects because they move around, and a chick would notice the movement. We'll use marbles, which will catch the light and glitter in the sun."

The team would also try using a red-tipped **syringe** filled with water. "Cranes are naturally attracted to the color red," Mr. Constantine explained. "Use the syringe to let a drip of water fall into the chick's mouth. Never squirt it in. That can hurt the chick."

A fourth technique would be to splash water into the chick's bowl from several feet up. The splashing water would make plenty of noise. Birds tend to be curious about moving water. When they hear it, they come over and look. The team would also give the chick a little pool to play in.

As the meeting came to a close, Mr. Constantine was full of encouragement. "Let's start with one technique this morning. If that doesn't work, we'll change our hypothesis and try something else. You never know what might do the trick!"

When a whooping crane hears moving water, it cannot help but go investigate.

BRINGING IN THE CLONES

Scientists are always trying to come up with new ways to save species from becoming extinct. One of the emerging theories is to **clone** a member of a species, or use **genes** to create an identical creature. Sometimes referred to as "de-extinction," this idea was introduced in stories and books such as Michael Crichton's *Jurassic Park.* While the concept has been in science fiction books for a long time, some experts believe it is soon going to be a reality.

Bringing back species that have disappeared is a goal that many scientists share. Others are not so sure this is the best idea. They worry that since the planet has moved on without these species, bringing them back might cause more problems than it will solve. Certainly, the idea is exciting, though. As Hank Greely, a **bioethicist** at Stanford University, recently said, "What intrigues me is just that it's really cool. A saber-toothed cat? It would be neat to see one of those."

CHAPTER 5

TAKING A DRINK

A wildlife center staff member keeps an
eye on Mabel from the blind.

Every day that week, Nathan greeted his dad at the front door with the
same question. "How is Mabel doing?" And to himself, Nathan wondered,
Was the experiment working? Which method was proving successful?
What if none of them worked?

Mr. Constantine made sure to keep his son updated on the team's
current hypothesis. The wildlife center staff tried one method after

another. They also tried combining two or more methods, trying to see what worked for Mabel. Each time an experiment proved one hypothesis wrong, the team thought of another. Nathan helped come up with ideas.

At first, there was little change in Mabel. Nathan was getting worried. Mr. Constantine was pretty worried, too. Would Mabel have to be brought in and fed by tubes?

After a few days, Mr. Constantine came through the front door with a big smile on his face. Nathan didn't need to ask his question. He already knew the answer. "You finally figured out what Mabel needed!" Nathan exclaimed.

The wildlife center staff watched for Mabel to become healthier and more active.

↰ Sometimes staff members visited Mabel or the other crane chicks in person for a closer look.

His father laughed. "It turns out, she really liked the splashing water," he said. "She'd follow the sound of it right to her pool. We also used the puppet to encourage her to dip her beak in. We finally watched her take a few sips."

"So, back to the scientific method," said Nathan seriously. "Step five is to analyze your test results. How did you do that?"

"We kept a close eye on her—how she acted, how she looked, whether she could drink water on her own," Mr. Constantine explained.

"And your conclusion?" prompted Nathan.

The wildlife center staff continued to keep a close eye on Mabel over the next few weeks.

"Mabel is so much better!" his father confirmed. "The splashing water and the puppet really worked. She took several drinks all on her own today. She is moving more and eating more, and the sparkle is back in her eyes already."

"Yes!" Nathan shouted, hopping up and down and throwing his arms in the air.

"Watch out, Nate," said Mr. Constantine with a chuckle. "If you act like that in front of the cranes, they might begin to think you're looking for a mate!"

SEEING BIRDS ON A STAMP

WILDLIFE CONSERVATION

WHOOPING CRANES

U.S. POSTAGE 3¢

In 1956, the U.S. Congress decided to put images of endangered animals on postage stamps. They hoped the stamps would help teach people about the risk facing these animals. A trio of three-cent stamps was published that year. One featured the wild turkey, one the pronghorn antelope, and the other the king salmon. All of these stamps were quite popular.

The following year, a fourth stamp was made. This one showed a family of whooping cranes. Bob Hines, an artist who worked for the U.S. Fish and Wildlife Service, created the image. It was the first stamp to use more than a single color. It used blue for the water, white for the two adult cranes, green for the grass, and orange for the pair of chicks by the mother bird's feet.

In late 1994, another stamp was issued with the whooping crane image. This stamp was designed to honor the wildlife conservation partnership between the United States and China. Zhan Gengxi of China created the delicate drawing, and Clarence Lee of Honolulu created the design and text.

GLOSSARY

artificially fertilize (ahr-tih-FISH-uh-lee FUR-tuh-lize) make able to produce babies through human-made means

bioethicist (bye-oh-EH-thi-sist) one who works with the moral complications of biological research

blind (BLYND) a shelter that is used to observe wildlife, without the animals knowing the observer is there

clone (KLOHN) to grow an identical plant or animal from the cells of another plant or animal

clutch (KLUHCH) a nest of eggs

crown (KROUN) the top part of something

dehydrated (dee-HYE-dray-tid) lacking enough water in your body for normal functioning

endangered (en-DAYN-jurd) at risk of becoming extinct, usually because of human activity

extinct (ik-STINGKT) no longer found alive; known about only through fossils or history

genes (JEENZ) the parts that make up chromosomes; genes are passed from parents to children and determine how you look and the way you grow

habitat (HAB-uh-tat) the place where an animal or a plant is usually found

hypothesis (hye-PAH-thi-sis) an idea that could explain how something works but must be proven by the scientific method

pesticides (PES-ti-sidez) chemicals used to kill pests such as insects

syringe (suh-RINJ) a tube with a plunger and a hollow needle, used for giving injections and drawing out blood or bodily fluids

FOR MORE INFORMATION

BOOKS

Gray, Susan. *Whooping Crane*. Ann Arbor, MI: Cherry Lake Publishing, 2008.

Harkins, Susan S., and William H. Harkins. *Threat to the Whooping Crane*. Hockessin, DE: Mitchell Lane, 2009.

Imbriaco, Alison. *The Whooping Crane: Help Save This Endangered Species!* Berkeley Heights, NJ: MyReportLinks.com, 2006.

McKenzie, Precious. *Whooping Cranes*. Vero Beach, FL: Rourke Publishing, 2010.

Shireman, Myrl. *Whooping Cranes*. Greensboro, NC: Mark Twain, 2013.

WEB SITES

BioKids: Critter Catalog—Whooping Crane

www.biokids.umich.edu/critters/Grus_americana

Learn more about whooping cranes, their habitats, and the challenges they face.

Environmental Education for Kids!—Whooping Crane

http://dnr.wi.gov/eek/critter/bird/crane.htm

Watch a video on the Whooping Crane Reintroduction Project.

International Crane Foundation—Whooping Crane

www.savingcranes.org/whooping-crane.html

Take a look at highlights from the Crane Chick Cam.

ABOUT THE AUTHOR

Tamra B. Orr is an author living in the Pacific Northwest. Orr has a degree in secondary education and English from Ball State University. She is the mother of four and the author of more than 350 books for readers of all ages. When she isn't writing or reading books, she is writing letters to friends all over the world. Although fascinated by all aspects of science, most of her current scientific method skills are put to use tracking down lost socks, missing keys, and overdue library books.